Mystery
of
His Will

*In memory of beloved sister **Leena D'Souza** of India, and dearest brother **Simate Brian Lisholo** of Zambia, devout saints who went to be with the Lord at the time of writing this book.*

Mystery of His Will

Printed in USA

A publication of Reflections *on* Faith

www.andrewcphiri.com | voiceoftheword@live.com

ISBN-13: 978-9982-9986-6-6

Unless otherwise indicated all scripture quotations were taken from the Holy Bible - King James Version © Cambridge University Press.

CREDITS: Image on page 115: Freepik.com, others from Wikimedia Commons.

FREE COPIES AVAILABLE WHILE STOCK LASTS

If you can't afford buying this book send a request for a free copy to voiceoftheword@live.com. However, please note that free copies can only be sent when resources are available.

Contents

1.

Past the boundary of time

*"He has also set eternity in the human heart;
yet no one can fathom what God has done
from beginning to end"*

Ecc. 3:11

The words you are now reading are held on paper, and the paper is held by your hand. You are held by where you are sitting right now, and whatever that is, it is held by the Earth. But, on what is the Earth resting? The inspired words of Scripture proclaimed that "*He stretcheth out the north over **the empty place**, and hangeth the earth upon nothing*" (Job 26:7).

In modern language we use the term Space to refer to the "*empty place*". And apart from the Earth, Space contains many other planets, and objects like stars and asteroids. All these objects, like the Earth, are also hanging upon "*nothing*". But note that Job used the word *nothing* in a general sense as we would use it in everyday communication. In reality however, Space is not *nothing*. It is actually a sea of particles; particles which are too small to be seen by our eyes. Thus, Space is a material thing and hence constitutes *something*!

Space is the theatre *room* where all the drama of the universe occurs. The word "occurs" is here being used with special care because it refers to a *happening*, a *movement* or a *manifestation* of something. How long it takes a happening, a movement, or a manifestation is what we call *Time*.

What you may immediately realise here is that Space and Time are inseparable: the coming into existence of Space was an event describable in terms of Time. It goes without saying that Time could not *be* if there was no occurrence of anything. Thus, there is Time because of Space, and Space can never be without Time. For this reason one can never accurately use Time to point to *when* Space began. Time and Space simply began in the same instance.

The coming into existence of Space and Time was *the beginning* of the material (or natural) world. However, as all things that begin to exist have a *cause,* the beginning of matter was preceded by the beginning of an entity called **the Word**, or **Logos**, which caused things into existence. This should lead us to distinguish between time for the material world and another for that spiritual dimension in which the Logos existed. *"All things were made by him* [the Word], *and without him was not any thing made that was made"* (Joh.1:2).

But what was the Word? What was this Logos?

To understand the Logos let us go on a journey back in Time, way back beyond what we described as *natural time*.

On this journey as we cross past the boundary of Time and Space we find ourselves in a dimension that cannot be described by natural laws of physics. It's a region unaffected by Time. It's a region that transcends Space. It is without beginning or end and is beyond the comprehension of our finite minds. But one thing we know is that it was and still is characterised by a supreme intelligence that caused all the laws of physics and the complex matter of the Universe.

Whichever *direction* one would look at in that timeless dimension he can only *see* the ever present 'I AM', not '*I was*' or '*I will be*'. History does not and cannot exist there! Actually, as we went past the boundary of Space and Time, the cool dew on the surface of our aircraft evaporated, with it our adjectives, nouns, verbs, and the entire language we would like to use to describe that timeless dimension! A dilemma: *How shall we tell the story about God when we get back to Earth?*

2.
Trapped in *form*

"For the invisible things of him from the creation of the world are clearly seen, being understood by the things that are made, even his eternal power and Godhead; so that they are without excuse"

Rom.1:20

Back on Earth our limited minds can hardly comprehend the Almighty God. What is more, we read in his Word that he has a son!

It was in the month of April in 2017 when I landed at *Ninoy Aquino International Airport* in Manila, the capital city of the Philippines. I was scheduled to minister at different churches in the country. Many memorable things occurred during the itinerary such as a strange and abrupt question I once experienced at a meal table.

The question was a probe into the meaning of "God" and "Son of God". I was sitting with different ministers around the table when someone asked: "Brother Andrew, is Jesus '*God*' or '*Son of God*'?"

It was not difficult to discern that the question did not arise from a desire to *learn* but to ignite an argument. I asked for some water to be poured in a glass which was on the table. Someone filled it quickly. I lifted the glass in my hands and asked:

"What am I holding in my hands?"

"Water!" came the answer. I continued:

"Will I be in order to dismiss your answer by saying, '*It's a glass I am holding and not water.*' Is it not true that for the convenience of language you have called the glass by the identity of the substance which now possesses it'"?

Is this '***water***' or '***a glass of water***'?

The carnal mind of man has difficulties in understanding God. God is invisible and everywhere. In that infinite state the finite mind of man cannot grasp or understand him. But he is gracious and desires to reveal himself to mankind. So God, "*at sundry times and **in divers manners**"*, spoke to man (Heb.1:1). The speaking of God isn't just through an audible voice or a spiritual vision. God reveals his greatness through the *form* (appearance or nature) of things he created. The great universe and wonders of nature testify about God. "*The heavens declare the glory of God; and the firmament showeth his handiwork*" wrote the psalmist. "*Day unto day uttereth speech, and night unto night showeth knowledge. There is no speech nor* *language, where their voice is not heard. Their line is gone out through all the earth, and their words to the end of the world*" (Psa.19:1-4).

Forms

Forms should point man to the reality of God but carnal man often finds himself lost in revering forms instead of the God of the forms. In Numbers 21:8 we read about how God commanded Moses to *form* a brazen serpent and lay it upon a pole. All the people who fell sick by snake-bites were to look upon it and get healed. *"It came to pass"*, the Scripture reads, *"that if a serpent had bitten any man, when he beheld the serpent of brass, he lived"* (v.9). That was God using a form to perform a work. He had a specific objective at that particular time. However, people got lost, missed the purpose and started to worship the brazen serpent! The form that was meant to point their faith to God was made to be God itself! That went on for a long time until one righteous and courageous man, Hezekiah, rose up to free people from their idolatry – *"He removed the high places, and brake the images, and cut down the groves, and brake in pieces the brazen serpent that Moses had made: for unto those days the children of*

Israel did burn incense to it: and he called it Nehushtan" (2 Kin.18:4).

"Nehushtan" means a piece of brass. Obviously there were people who felt Hezekiah disrespected Moses by breaking the image and calling it a mere piece of metal. However, those with eyes to see should have known that the God who spoke to Moses was the same one who used Hezekiah. It is important to understand that God had used that object as a way for carnal man – a *being* trapped in a body of flesh by which he relates with the physical world through the senses of *sight, touch, smell, hearing*, and *taste* – to look at something and then direct their faith to God the healer.

In the Old Testament we find more other rituals and holy places to which man's mind looked in trying to revere God. However, the forms of activities or words of the Law pointed to the coming of the real thing. The *real thing* is not the *form* or *mask* through which God manifested but the very Spirit of God himself! It had always been God's desire for man to reach the place where he could worship him as he is – a spirit being, not attached to form or a place. When the Samaritan woman talked about some 'right place' where worship ought to be done the Lord Jesus answered her, "*Woman, believe me, the hour cometh, when ye shall* **neither in this mountain, nor yet at Jerusalem, worship the Father***. Ye worship ye know not what: we know what we worship: for salvation is of the Jews. But the hour cometh, and now is, when* **the true worshippers shall worship the Father in spirit and in truth***: for the Father seeketh such to worship him. God is a Spirit: and* **they that worship him must worship him in spirit and in truth***"* (Joh.4:21-24).

A person who receives the revelation of truth gets liberated from the imprisonment of forms. *"Ye shall know the truth, and the truth shall make you free"*, the Lord said (Joh.8:32).

Lost in *forms* of words

Now 'forms' can be images of things which people worship as idols but they can also be *words* or *phrases*.

Words and phrases are vehicles through which truth can be conveyed but yet are not *themselves* the truth! The vehicle may even be faulty whilst the truth it carries is correct.

To understand the Godhead one needs more than the vehicle of letters, words or semantics. Therein lies the trap for theologians. They look into Scripture and theorize three persons in the Godhead. They call the persons *God the Father, God the Son,* and *God the Holy Spirit*. This is a direct contradiction to this command which was given to the Hebrews: *"Hear, O Israel: The LORD **our God is one LORD**"* (Deu.6:4). And contrary to the idea that God the Father is sitting *with* the Son and the Holy Spirit is also *besides* him, Yahweh declares *"I am the LORD, and there is none else, **there is no God beside me**"* (Isa.45:5). But so confident are Trinitarians at their doctrine that they even refer to Jesus, or the Holy Spirit, or the Father, as *a* member, *a* portion, or *a third* of the Godhead! Again that contradicts the scripture which says, *"In Him* [Jesus] *dwelleth **all the fullness** [not a part or a third] of the Godhead bodily"* (Col.2:9).

Those with eyes to see should perceive that there is and has always been **ONE Almighty Spirit who is *everywhere* and has neither beginning nor end**. However, note that before anything was created he could not be called *God*. God is something that is worshipped but there were no angels or man to worship him. But even if angels or human beings were created, how would they ever relate with, or comprehend, such an eternal being which was not confined to Space and Time?

The almighty invisible Spirit had to manifest in ***form*** in order to relate in Space and Time. The form was the first thing to proceed from the Almighty Spirit and thus was the beginning of Time as the *Alpha* (Isa.44:6).

The Alpha was not 'another God' but **a visible 'mask' of the invisible Spirit** through which he would create and relate with everything. In the future, Time will wind up and end in him as the *Omega*. Thus, whenever God in Scripture is referred to as the Alpha and Omega, that is a description of his being in Time, not Eternity.

The visible mask was *"**the angel of his** [invisible] **presence**"* (Isa.63:9). It was that mask, the first thing to be created by God, which began to speak, *"let there be…!"* and things began to come into existence (Joh.1:1-3, Rev.3:14, Pro.8:22-24). It was through that mask that angels and human beings could look at God. So, although *"no man has seen God **at any time**"* (Joh.1:18), it was that mask – which sometimes appeared like an angel, like a human being, like a fire, like a cloud, like a light – that the prophets of old looked at, and for the limitation or convenience of language and communication, declared that they had seen God: *"Then went up Moses, and Aaron, Nadab and Abihu, and seventy of the elders of Israel **and they saw the God of Israel**, and there was **under His feet** as it*

were a paved work of a sapphire stone"
(Exo.24:9-10).

May I state here that when God manifested in a light or a cloud, the light or cloud was not God, but for the convenience of language and communication, a person could say, "I have seen God"! Even when God took on the form of dust and appeared like a human being to Abraham, that visible form of dust was not God. It was only a form through which the invisible God had manifested. But in language we may still say, God "*appeared*" to Abraham (Gen.18:1). Likewise, when we come into the New Testament the same thing happened. However, in the New Testament God no longer appeared in **temporal** manifestations of light, cloud, or angelic form. In the New Testament Yahweh "*prepared*" a **permanent** form of human body through which to manifest (Heb.10:5).

When that body was thirty years old it was ready to be filled by God's Spirit and be used as the image of the invisible God. This is what Matthew wrote about the event of the baptism of Jesus: "*And Jesus, when he was baptized, went up straightway out of the water: and, lo, the heavens were opened unto him, and he saw the Spirit of God descending like a dove, and lighting upon him. And lo a voice from heaven, saying, This is my beloved Son, in*

whom *I am well pleased*" (3:16-17). Yes, the Spirit of God was pleased to dwell in Jesus; he was *"**the image of the invisible God**"* (Col.1:15, cf. Heb.1:1-3).

So, it should be clear now that when we refer to Jesus as God, the way Thomas did in John 20:28, we are referring to him as the manifestation of God in flesh. Like in the words of Paul to Timothy, *"great is the mystery of godliness: **God was manifest in the flesh**, justified in the Spirit, seen of angels, preached unto the Gentiles, believed on in the world, received up into glory"* (1 Tim.3:16). And we are *"looking for that blessed hope, and the glorious **appearing of the great God** and our saviour Jesus Christ"* (Tit.2:13, Isa.43:11).

But this far in this message important questions may still linger in our minds: Why did God step *out* of Eternity *into* Time? Why did he further give us his son? Why didn't he just remain 'alone' in Eternity? Some people go further to suggest that had God left things as they were (i.e. without creating the world) there would have never been evil and all the sufferings we go through! So, what really was God's will or intention for all the drama we see in this world? Let us go on this intriguing journey of faith and behold the unfolding mystery of his will!

3.

Counsel of his will

*"And God said, Let there be light: and
there was light.
And God saw the light, that it was good:
and God divided the light from the darkness"*

Gen.1:3-4

In Eternity, when nothing had been created, the Almighty Spirit was alone with his thoughts. He was all-knowing and therefore present everywhere, the *all in all*.

Being present everywhere there was no way anything (whether existing as a concept, a potential or an actual thing) could exist outside him! Every conceivable thing, whether good or evil, could only potentially exist within him – "*The eyes of the LORD are in every place, beholding the evil and the good*" (Pro.15:3, cf. Heb.4:13). In the words of the psalmist, "*If I ascend up into heaven, thou art there: if I make my bed in hell, behold, thou art there*" (Psa.139:8).

The great Eternal Spirit stepped into Time to:
1) Cause the Good and the Evil to manifest.
2) Preserve the Good, and;
3) Annihilate the Evil.

In Time, all those through whom the Good would manifest shall live and abide forever with it: "*According as he hath chosen us in him before the foundation of the world, that we should be holy and without blame before him in love*" (Eph.1:4). Likewise, "*the children of disobedience*" (Eph.2:2), being vessels through which Evil would express itself, shall be annihilated with it, *"reserved unto fire against the day of judgment and perdition of ungodly men"* (2 Pet.3:7, Jud.1:6, Rev.20:14-15). Right from the beginning the first man had been warned about this fate of death – *"in the day that thou eatest thereof thou shalt surely die"* (Gen.2:17).

When Time shall wind up into Eternity, and Jesus Christ would have handed over all things to the Creator, God will return to being the *"all in all"* (1 Cor.15:28) but with 'future-eternity' only having the *potential* of Good!

In all this we behold and revere the sovereignty of the Creator. He is God, ***"declaring the end from the beginning***, *and from ancient times the things that are not yet done,* **saying, My counsel shall stand**, *and I will do all my pleasure"* (Isa.46:10). Even before the foundations of the world he had already purposed the death and resurrection of Jesus Christ, for in the revelation given to John we read that he was the Lamb slain *"from the foundation of the world"* (Rev.13:8).

God's work from the beginning shows his ultimate intention to manifest the Good and Evil, to preserve the Good and destroy Evil: in Genesis we read that in the beginning he *"divided the light from the darkness"* (Gen.1:4), and in Isaiah 45:7 God said, *"I form the light, and create darkness: I make peace, and create evil: I the LORD do all these things*".

But, why didn't the Almighty Spirit leave things as they were, to continue 'existing' only as *potentials*, a state in which no actual evil would have occurred?

The Price of God's Desire

Well, had the Almighty left 'things' as they were there also wouldn't have been actual *good!* And if a *good* thing forever remains a thought its value shall likewise remain *unmanifest* and unrealised and that would amount to being *nothing* and meaningless! So, it was not good for God to remain *alone* with his thoughts.

The story of redemption in the Bible shows that God desired to bring Good to reality. "*And God said, 'Let there be light, and there was light and God saw the light that it was good: and God divided the light from the darkness*" (Gen.1:3-4). The manifestation of Good was not to be for the mere sake of it; God had a desire to have a family of beings that he could fellowship with in love. Now therein lay the challenge: love can only be true when the entities involved in a relationship also have a real choice to *hate*. This required God to create beings that would be endowed with *free will*.

Here I want to emphasise that the granting of free will comes with it the possibility of evil because there can never be true choice until one is truly free to do good or evil. Thankfully however, when evil manifests that provides a way for it to be dealt with!

Now God is so great that he could take a 'piece' out of himself, so to speak, and create another being which could think, reason, and make independent decisions. How he was able to do that when he created angels and human beings is perhaps the most mysterious thing he ever did! It's simply beyond our comprehension. Some overzealous scientists believe that they too will one day be able to repeat the feat by creating a self-conscious computer, a machine that will be able to reason beyond its coded instructions. Today millions of dollars are being invested in the development of *artificial intelligence* (AI) systems. But although current AI systems are able to do some amazing things, they are light-years behind to catch up with the real intelligence of human beings, and they are nowhere near the possibility of possessing free will!

Great as it was to create beings with free will, as has been earlier alluded to, the work was done at a risky price of also permitting evil.

"What if man foolishly chooses to despise the will and love of his creator and becomes a danger to himself and other creatures around him?" If you were with God in his counsel of thoughts, how would you have handled this question? The biggest 'dilemma' in this whole drama would be that if man chooses Evil over Good, he would put himself on the path to destruction because by doing wrong man would have freely chosen to become a vessel of Evil, a thing which God had purposed to annihilate!

Well, the problem wasn't as complex for God. He provided an opportunity for man to *fail*, *learn*, and then *repent*! So, instead of creating a world of automated beings, beings which would automatically do good and hence be not real, because free will provided an opportunity to learn its price was worth it!

Learning

One day my little child saw me eating what looked like sweet tomato sauce. He saw the red bottle and was sure it is what he had once tasted. Unknown to him it was chilli sauce that I was eating. He begged me to give him some. He could not believe whatever explanation I gave him and so he started crying for it. He doubted my care and love for him, so to speak. He thought I was hiding something better from him. Well, there was a way to let him *learn* the truth about the matter. I had to let him taste (experience) what he craved for in hope that he would learn and make a wise decision. I knew that he would spew out the sauce and that would be a waste or loss of something that costed money to buy. The act would amount to subjecting the boy to what some may consider a vain exercise. "Vain" because after giving him the sauce it would be spewed out. However, the 'vanity' or 'loss' was for a greater purpose – learning!

When the fall occurred in the beginning God permitted all creation to come under 'vanity' in hope of later bringing deliverance to all those who would learn and repent. Is it not written that *"they hated knowledge, and did not choose the fear of the LORD:* ***They would none of my counsel****: they despised all my reproof.* ***Therefore shall they eat of the fruit of their own way****, and be filled with their own devices"* (Pro.1:29-31)? And elsewhere again it is declared that ***"the creature was made subject to vanity****, not willingly, but* ***by*** *reason of him who hath subjected the same in hope, Because the creature itself also shall be delivered from the bondage of corruption into the glorious liberty of the children of God*" (Rom.8:20-21).

4.

Thy will be done

"Jesus saith unto them, My meat is to do the will of him that sent me, and to finish his work"

Joh.4:34

Only God is omnipresent, omniscient, and omnipotent.

Omnipresent is a state of being everywhere. *Omniscient* is a state of knowing everything. *Omnipotent* means being all powerful.

The will of a being which knows everything (past, present or future) and is thus everywhere, and which is all powerful to do anything, can never be anything short of perfect. If it is such a being which created us, his counsel ought to be heeded to with all faith. When he speaks, all of his creation ought to be still and listen. Listening and following his words would be life, and doing anything otherwise would be fatal. That is what Yahweh is, and in the beginning mankind was foolish enough to prefer his own way over God's way of the *Tree of Life*!

Mankind rejecting the way *of* the Tree of Life

The woman, a created being, was foolish enough to listen to the Serpent, another created being, which suggested to her that God was hiding something better from mankind. Adam, a son of God, was not deceived (1 Tim.2:14). He identified with his wife's sin in order to save her from the wrath of God.

Mankind's disobedience was an act of unbelief in God's counsel. God's counsel was perfect and man should have used it to live his life and govern the Earth. When man rejected that perfect will, God closed the way of the Tree of Life to let him fully partake of the fruit of his choice - *"They would none of my counsel: they despised all my reproof.* ***Therefore shall they eat of the fruit of their own way****, and be filled with their own devices."* God *"placed at the east of the garden of Eden Cherubims, and a flaming sword which turned every way to keep* ***the way of the tree of life****"* (Gen.3:24).

Earth left to man's will

With the way of the Tree of Life (God's perfect will) closed on Earth, it only had full pre-eminence in Heaven where all spiritual beings are fully yielded to God's will; in Revelation 2:7 John tells us of *"the Tree of Life which is in the midst of the paradise of God"*. Down here, the Earth was left to be ruled by man's way. However, mankind, through his disobedient act of preferring to yield to Satan's counsel rather than God's, had actually passed the rulership of the world to the hands of that wicked angel! It is for this reason that Satan was able to tell the Lord Jesus that *"all this power... **is delivered unto**"* *me, and to whomsoever I will I give it"* (Luk.4:6).

With the world having actually been delivered into Satan's hands, he has been using his wicked people to control it. It is for this reason that *"the whole creation groaneth and travaileth in pain together until now"* (Rom.8:22). The terrible condition of the world will only end when creation is delivered back to God's children, for *"the earnest expectation of the creature waiteth for the manifestation of the sons of God"* (Rom.8:19).

Fruits of the way of man's will

From the time mankind chose to follow his own will, the fruits of **the will of his flesh** have been continuously evil: In the entire world ***"the works of the flesh are manifest,*** *which are these adultery, fornication, uncleanness, lasciviousness, idolatry, witchcraft, hatred, variance, emulations, wrath, strife, seditions, heresies, envyings, murders, drunkness, [and] revellings"* (Gal.5:19).

All who are vessels through which these evil attributes manifest shall not have any part of eternal life. Eternal life shall be given to those chosen to live forever when Evil would have been destroyed in Hell. *"As I have also told you in time past"* Paul reminded the Galatians, *"they which do such things shall not inherit the kingdom of God"* (Gal.5:21). Only those who live by the will of God shall live forever - *"The world passeth away, and the lust thereof, but **he that doeth the will of God abideth forever**"* (1 Joh.2:17).

The way opened to the Tree of Life

About 2000 years ago, a great event happened on Earth. God prepared himself a body through which he would manifest. God would no longer be perceived like some distant supernatural being who was unaware of the difficulties people had in obeying his will. He would now be Emmanuel – *"God with us"* (Mat.1:23)!

God's act of manifesting in the flesh was as though to demonstrate that if he were a human himself and someone else was God, he would still have chosen to eat of and live by the will of his creator!

The one important thing the life of Jesus demonstrated to us was walking in the perfect will of God. He could do nothing but what God revealed to him - *"Then answered Jesus and said unto them, Verily, verily, I say unto you, The Son can do nothing of himself, but what he seeth the Father do: for what things soever he doeth, these also doeth the Son likewise*" (Joh.5:19).

Unlike the modern strange Gospel which enthuses people to pursue desires of their will, the Lord Jesus taught us to pray for the restoration of the will of God to Earth - "*After this manner therefore pray ye…Thy will be done in earth, as it is in heaven*" (Mat.6:10). Even in moments of extreme pain and agony the Lord showed us that God's will was more important. "*Father*", he prayed, "*if thou be willing, remove this cup from me: nevertheless not my will, but thine, be done*" (Luk.22:42).

Unlike the "*first Adam*" who ate of the forbidden tree, the "*last Adam*" chose to eat of the will of God only. "*My meat*", he said, *"is to do the will of him that sent me, and to finish his work"* (Joh.4:34). To a group of Jews who one day wanted to lay their hands on him to kill him he said, "*I seek not mine own will, but the will of the Father which hath sent me*" he said (Joh.5:30).

The coming of Jesus was the opening of the way to eternal life. "*I am the WAY, the TRUTH, and the LIFE*" He said (Joh.14:6). Yes, he is the only way of Truth which gives life. "*For God so loved the world, that he gave his only begotten Son, that whosoever believeth in him should not perish, but have **everlasting life**" (Joh.3:16). In the beginning mankind had followed another way of deceit which led to death but through Christ mankind has an opportunity to repent and partake of the Tree of Life which is the source of eternal life.

5.

Born again *to* the will of God

"The wind bloweth where it listeth, and thou hearest the sound thereof, but canst not tell whence it cometh, and wither it goeth; so is every one that is born of the Spirit"

Joh.3:8

"The hour is come, that the Son of man should be glorified. Verily, verily, I say unto you, Except a corn of wheat fall into the ground and die, it abideth alone: but if it die, it bringeth forth much fruit" (Joh.12:23-24). Jesus was the first seed to be sown in death in order to bring forth many *seeds* (sons of God).

A person becomes a son of God when he or she gets *born again*. The new birth experience involves being filled with the Holy Spirit. This Holy Spirit comes, not just to make someone speak in tongues or experience an emotion but, to lead a person into **the truth of the will of God**: *"Howbeit when he, **the Spirit of truth**, is come, he **will guide you into all truth**"* (Joh.16:13). The born-again experience causes a person to stop relying on what his mind can fathom or predict about a situation or decision; with his mind yielded to the Holy Spirit, he or she will hear the leading of the Spirit and move with it. Like the Lord illustrated, *"The wind bloweth where it listeth, and thou hearest the sound thereof, but canst not tell whence it cometh, and wither it goeth; so is every one that is born of the Spirit"* (Joh.3:8).

What we see in all this is that the born again experience is really about being born to the will of God. And just as man who is "born of the will *of* the flesh" lives by the will of the flesh, so those who get "born of the will of God" live by the will of God - *"But as many as received Him, to them gave He power **to become the sons of God**, even to them that believe on His name: **Which were born**, **not** of blood, nor **of the will of the flesh**, nor of the will of man, **but of God**"* (Joh.1:12-13). It is only when we are born again to walk in the will of God that we can truly be in the family of Christ for the Lord himself said, *"**whosoever shall do the will of my Father** which is in heaven, **the same is my brother**, and sister, and mother"* (Mat.12:50).

Following God's will is a rest

Being led by the Spirit involves ceasing from the strivings of your mind and letting God be in control; *"Thou hast delivered me from **the strivings of the people**"*, the psalmist said (Psa.18:43).

Sons of God do not strive in their minds, they rest in prayer and wait on the Lord. They also don't strive to live holy because their righteousness is not by their works. They are dead to the flesh and so the Holy Spirit lives freely in them to do Good. For *"they that are Christ's have crucified the flesh with the affections and lusts"* (Gal.5:24).

Watchman Nee had something important to say about the rest that the Holy Spirit gives:

*The Christian life from start to finish is based upon this principle of utter dependence upon the Lord Jesus…To sit down is simply to rest our whole weight - our load, ourselves, our future, everything – upon the Lord. We let him bear the responsibility and cease to carry it ourselves…How can I receive the power of the Spirit for service? Must I labor for it? Must I plead with God for it? Must I afflict my soul by fastings and self-denials to merit it? Never! That is not the teaching of Scripture…How did we receive the forgiveness of our sins? …**Because Jesus died on the Cross my sins are forgiven; because he is exalted to the throne I am endued with power from on high**. The one gift is no more dependent than the other upon what I am or what I do. I did not merit forgiveness and neither do I merit the gift of the Spirit.*[1]

It is only when we rest in the hands of God that we can become his "*workmanship*" (Eph.2:10), i.e. a piece of work that he can break and mold (Jer.18:4).

A prophetic word given to William Branham

The Bride of Christ will have to be one with her husband before she can be raptured.

---

[1] In *Sit, Walk, Stand*, p.3-6,CLC Publications © 1957

She has to be one *in his will*. Yes, that time is coming when our husband shall say, 'that is bone of my bones' (Eph.5:30). It thus goes without saying that no one who is given to the cares of life and who has no personal relationship with Christ shall have a part in the Rapture.

The Ice, the Water, the Fire

In the Rapture God will only take those that are worthy to rule the coming world in the Millennium. The Millennium will be the third and final time the Earth will experience a new beginning.

In the prehistoric era when angels were given to rule over the world of apes and dinosaurs evil occurred when Lucifer craved to rule after his will (Eze.28:13-15, Isa.14:12-15). He misgoverned the Earth and God halted the world by glaciation. The planet froze as fog covered the atmosphere. Great darkness filled the Earth. But God had purposed not to make a full end and so, after a long period of time, he started a new beginning (read Jer.4:23-27).

"Let there be Light!" God commanded and it was so. The planet got restored and this time it was put in the hands of mankind. That was the first new beginning. However, in the

new world mankind too chose his way over the will of God. The results of man's ways were disastrous. *"The wickedness of man was great in the earth, and that every imagination of the thoughts of his heart was only evil continually"* (Gen.6:5). That antediluvian era was destroyed by floods of water. Only Noah and his sons and their wives survived. After the water sunk into the Earth a testimony of huge bodies of water called oceans remain to this day. These waters cover 75% of the Earth!

All human races today descended from the three sons of Noah. Man hasn't learned a single lesson; his faulty *will* still reigns and through it the world has become laden with sickness, wars, and depression. It's a world characterized by adultery, fornication, uncleanness, lasciviousness, idolatry, witchcraft, hatred, variance, emulations, wrath, strife, seditions, heresies, envyings, murders, drunkness, and revellings. These evils have passed from one country's culture to another.

In this modern era of satellite technology evil has had a seamless flow through television and the Internet. But prophecy tells us that this sin-sick world, together with the satellites that litter the heavens, will one day be destroyed and cleansed with fire. The destruction of this present world will not be by ice or water but by fire – *"the heavens shall pass away with a great noise, and the elements shall melt with fervent heat, the earth also and the works that are therein shall be burned up"* (2 Pet.3:10). Dearly beloved, isn't the current heating up of our planet an early warning of the destruction that is to come? Well, all those who are yielded to the wonderful, good, and perfect will of God need not to worry or panic because they are promised another new beginning that shall one day dawn on this earth. That will be the third and last new beginning which shall be headed by God himself through Jesus Christ.

What will all the three new beginnings be but to show that order, blessings, and joy can only be a reality when we live by the will and knowledge of that omniscient creator? Yes, there shall be joy and true prosperity in that new world because the knowledge of God shall fill the Earth (Isa.11:9). In that new world everything will revolve around the way of the Tree of Life, which is the perfect will of God - *"And he showed me a pure river of water of life, clear as crystal, proceeding out of the throne of God and of the Lamb. In the midst of the street of it, and on either side of the river, was there the tree of life, which bare twelve manner of fruits, and yielded her fruit every month: and the leaves of the tree were for the healing of the nations"* (Rev.22:1-2).

Candidates of the Rapture

In this present world we are tested to live and walk by his will. Remember that the whole world was once perfect as long as everything lived in the due order of God's will. Everything was in its place and there was a place for everything. Man had lived by EVERY word that proceeded from the mouth of his creator. Mankind was not to live by some of God's Word but by EVERY WORD AS A WHOLE! Anything short of that would result into death. That is how crucial and important the way of God's will is. At the same time it's so simple that all one has to do is to rest in what God has said and there will be all the security and peace – *"Come unto me, all ye that labour and are heavy laden, and **I will give you rest**. Take my yoke upon you, and learn of me; for I am meek and lowly in heart: and ye shall find rest unto your souls. For **my yoke is easy, and my burden is light**"* (Mat.11:28-29).

"Those in the Bride do only His will"

One day William Branham had a vision in which he saw the healing of a sick child. In the vision he saw himself in a small house. He saw details of how the house looked and the different people in it and the sick child. There was a dark-haired woman in her early twenties who leaned her head against the kitchen door. To his left was an older woman who was crying. He saw the old woman taking off her glasses and wiping them with her handkerchief. To his right was a young man with blond hair. He also saw how terribly afflicted the sick child was. Then the angel asked William Branham: "Have the father bring the boy to you so that you can pray for him and he'll live."

It was not long after the vision ended that someone knocked on the door calling for prayers. When brother Branham went to the house it was exactly as he had seen in the vision. The blond-haired young man was there. The young woman was there. He got so excited at this and asked for the child to be brought to him to be prayed for. But to his surprise, when he prayed the child got sicker and was almost dying. Something wasn't right! As he looked around in the house he noticed something was missing – the old woman who had taken off her glasses in the vision! As he thought on this thing the blond-haired young man was about to leave. Brother Branham got worried. He asked God to forgive him. As he looked over the window of the house, there was an old woman coming to the house. She was the grandmother to the sick child. He knew she was the one he had seen in the vision. She entered the house. When she asked about the child, the mother said he was dying as she cried whilst leaning her head against the kitchen door. Brother Branham could now see that the whole setting was exactly as he had seen in the vision. He now waited for the part of the grandmother sitting down in a chair and wiping her glasses. Well, it happened just like that! The glasses had fogged and so she took them off and started wiping them. At that brother Branham asked for the child to be given again to him. He prayed and the miracle happened!

Dear friend, before the Rapture we all have to learn how to live by THUS SAITH THE LORD. We can only be united with him in that great catching away when we become one with him in his will. That is exactly what God revealed to brother Branham at another time. The Holy Spirit told him to pick up a pen and write these words:

Jesus never did anything until it was first showed Him by the Father (Joh.5:19). This harmony is now to exist between the Groom and His bride. He shows her His Word of life. She receives it. She never doubts it...She *performs the command of the Word in His name for she has 'THUS SAITH THE LORD'…**Those in the bride do only His will**.* *No one can make them do otherwise.* ***They have 'THUS SAITH THE LORD' or they keep still.***[2]

Oh saints, the time is late and we ought to walk circumspectly, redeeming the time for the days are evil!

The sum of the matter

The Bible opens and closes with the story of the Tree of Life. In the beginning when man sinned the way *of* the Tree of Life was closed (Gen.2:9, 3:24). The Bible ends with the restoration of the tree to Earth and how its leaves will be for the healing of the nations (Rev.22:2). Here is the sum of the matter we have shared this far:

1) In the beginning mankind chose his will over God's perfect will. In doing that mankind despised the provided *"way of the Tree of Life"*. God closed his way (Gen.3:24).

2) In closing the way of the Tree of Life God withdrew his perfect will from the earth

---

[2] In *Exposition of the Seven Church Ages*, p.172. Voice of God Recordings © 2005

and left human beings to *"eat of the fruit of their own way"* (Pro.1:29-31).

3) Later God manifested in flesh as though to demonstrate that if he were a human being himself and someone else was God, he would have chosen to eat of and live by the will of his creator. *"Then said he, Lo, I come to do thy will, O God"* (Heb.10:9). *"Jesus saith unto them, My meat is to do the will of him that sent me, and to finish his work"* (Joh.4:34).

4) Our prayer in life should be the restoration of the will of God to Earth. *"After this manner therefore pray ye...Thy will be done in earth, as it is in heaven"* (Mat.6:10).

5) Through Jesus Christ many other sons of God have been born to the will of God – *"But as many as received Him, to them gave he power to become the sons of God, even to them that believe on His name: Which were born, not of blood, nor of the will of the flesh, nor of the will of man, but of God"* (Joh.1:12-13). We get born again to the will of God!

6) Those who have chosen their will over God's will are the *"children of disobedience"* (Eph.2:2) and they shall die. Those who have been restored to the will of God shall live

forever.

Despite all this profoundness of God's will, we find ourselves living in a time of a strange Gospel which enthuses people to pursue the will of their minds. It is a gospel that subtly influences people to think that their will is actually God's will.

6.

My will be done

"Not everyone that saith unto me, Lord, Lord, shall enter into the kingdom of heaven but he that doeth the will of my father which is in heaven. Many will say to me in that day, Lord, Lord, have we not prophesied in thy name? and in thy name have cast out devils? And in thy name done many wonderful works? And then will I profess unto them, I never knew you: depart from me, ye that work iniquity"

Mat.7:21-23

Behold we have a new perverted 'Gospel'. It is not based on "Thy will be done" but "my will be done"!

It is important to know that the ministry of Jesus Christ was centred on following God's will. The Lord's ministry was never about fulfilling his ambition. The Lord was always concerned about fulfilling his father's will: *"Verily, verily, I say unto you"*, he said, *"The Son can do nothing of himself, but what he seeth the Father do"* (Joh.5:19). Paul admonished believers saying, *"Set your affection on things above, not on things on the earth. For ye are dead, and your life is hid with Christ in God"* (Col.3:2-3).

A new agenda

The modern perverted Gospel has a different agenda. The agenda is not heavenward; it's downward, a worldly agenda. The agenda attempts to put the will of man at the center of God's programme. When you closely look at it however, it is not difficult to see that it has never been God's programme; it has been man's ambitious programme masquerading as a divine programme!

The new Gospel excites people to discover their 'self' and encourages them to enforce their desires with a strong will. It emphasizes that "where there is a will there is a way!" The "way" being spoken of is not that of the Lord but what a person's mind can conceive. The new Gospel is all about having confidence in yourself. It is so contrary to the true Gospel of Christ which requires that we "*worship God in the spirit...and **have no confidence in the flesh**"* (Phi.3:3). The true Gospel of Christ is not about gain but loss. Like Paul testified, "*what things were gain to me, those I counted loss for Christ*" (Col.3:7).

The true Gospel is about seeking spiritual things; it's about seeking God and asking, 'Where is the Lord?' It's about seeking God whilst he may be found, before the Grace period runs out. "*Seek ye the LORD while he may be found, call ye upon him while he is near*" the Spirit said through Isaiah; "*Let the wicked **forsake his way**, and the unrighteous man **his thoughts**: and let him return unto the LORD, and he will have mercy upon him; and to our God, for he will abundantly pardon. For **my thoughts are not your thoughts, neither are your ways my ways, saith the LORD**. For as the heavens are higher than the earth, so are my ways higher than your ways, and my thoughts than your thoughts*" (Isa.55:6-9). Yes, a true believer's way of life is to forsake his way and thoughts and seek the "higher" thoughts of God. But beware, it has always been Satan's tactic to make people afraid of seeking God's way. Such believers get trapped in the fear of thinking that God's way may not be so pleasant. However, those who have tasted God's good will know the truthfulness of this promise of God: *"For **I know the thoughts that I think toward you**, saith the LORD, **thoughts of peace**, and not of evil, **to give you an expected end**. Then shall ye call upon me, and ye shall go and pray unto me, and I will hearken unto you. And **ye shall seek me, and find me**, when ye shall search for me with all your heart"* (Jer.29:11-13).

Enemies of the Cross

Although many self-proclaimed modern apostles and prophets claim to be in the ministry of winning souls for Christ, it only takes a little discernment for anyone to see that they are actually in business. Like apostle Paul warned in his letter to the Philippians, their true god is their belly and their focus is on earthly things – *"For many walk, of whom I have told you often, and now tell you even weeping, that they are the enemies of the cross of Christ: Whose end is destruction, **whose God is their belly**, and whose glory is in their shame, **who mind earthly things**"* (Phi.3:18-19). And yes, they glory in things that true saints consider to be shameful. But why should someone glory in a shameful thing? Well, when a mind gets seared with a hot iron of deceit, no decency is left in it (1 Tim.4:2).

Making merchandise of people

Apostle Peter once gave a strong warning about false prophets and teachers who would arise in the future. Today we see all his words fulfilling before us, especially in charismatic churches. Here is the prophetic message Peter gave: *"But there were false prophets also among the people, even as there shall be false teachers among you, who privily shall bring in damnable heresies, even denying the Lord that bought them, and bring upon themselves swift destruction. And many shall follow their **pernicious ways**; by reason of whom the way of truth shall be evil spoken of. And through **covetousness** shall they with **feigned words** make **merchandise** of you: whose judgment now of a long time lingereth not, and their damnation slumbereth not"* (2 Pet.2:1-2).

Note the following important words Peter used:

Pernicious

Being pernicious means "having a harmful effect, especially in a gradual or subtle way." Isn't that exactly what has happened to Christianity? In a gradual manner wrong practices and deceptive doctrines entered the church.

It started with someone saying, "It's the heart which matters and not how we dress outwardly" and before we knew it women now dress tight and revealing outfits in churches. In a gradual manner Gospel music started adopting worldly rhythms until the good old time spiritual hymns got replaced with *boogie woogie* and *Rock n' Roll*! And talking about preachers, they quote Malachi 3:8 to warn people about the importance of giving to the Lord when it's really their pleasurable life that poor people in a congregation are financing. Talk of being subtle! Their deception is causing people of the world to despise and insult what should be sacred things of God.

Covetousness

To be covetous is to have a great desire to possess something which belongs to someone else. When you look at the opulent lifestyles of many modern preachers, you will see that they are trying to acquire the status of a celebrity. They want to dress, talk, and be guarded like some big person. They crave for importance. These same preachers also have juniors under them who crave to behave and dress just like them. It's a whole brood of vipers characterized by a deep thirst for wealth, pride and prominence.

Feigned words

To feign is to "pretend to be affected by a feeling, state, or injury". Isn't that what we often see when a charismatic preacher adds drama to his voice when trying to show that he is speaking under the anointing? The preacher may scream, jump or utter words in an emotional tone to act as though he is being prompted by the Spirit of God. However, the preacher's drama is only meant to manipulate people's emotions to yield to his pleas. The animal on the pulpit is nothing more than a sensational actor.

Merchandise

Merchandise refers to "goods to be bought and sold". That is what people in congregations of prosperity preachers have been reduced to. What you see as a 'mega church' is actually huge stock!

The Prosperity Gospel originated from the West but Africa has adopted it. In Africa Nigerians have become very good at it. Big Nigerian preachers have mastered and evolved the trick. They are spreading their influence and enriching themselves by going beyond the borders of their country. The preacher plants a church in another country and then implements a system wherein he sends his stooge to pastor it. The stooge has to be a Nigerian. At the core of this strategy is to have a trusted person who can collect monies and faithfully channel them to the headquarters. This has become an enterprise with sophisticated marketing skills: prophecies, psychological tricks, and miracles are crafted to attract crowds.

When foreign visitors visit the headquarter-church of "papa", great entertainment awaits them, at their cost! There is a restaurant waiting for them which is owned by the church. The visitor also has to return home with souvenirs of books on topics of "faith", "healing", and the "anointing". The books are ofcourse written by the "papa". No, they don't get the books for free; they have to buy them from a bookshop owned by the church. And then there is also anointing oil or holy water to be bought. This anointed stuff can be used on their business properties, their homes, or even on their bodies, for the favour of God to manifest in their lives. Oh, what a sham!

The selling of the so-called 'anointing oil' or 'holy water' has become widespread in Africa. People are paraded to give testimonies of what the oil did for them. Unknown to most ignorant people is the fact that those testimonies are meant to translate to more sales of the 'miracle products'. Talk of advertising skills in charismatic churches! It's a whole new fraudulent industry. Listen, any preacher who begs for money for his ministry is not called of God! When God calls a person he raises people who will give out of their own free will to support the ministry. No true ministry of God emphasises on giving. True ministers proclaim and teach the Gospel of the kingdom and God takes care of the rest.

Well, in all this confusion we are comforted to know that what God offers is free, it is *without money and without price*!

7.

Without money and
without price

"Wherefore do ye spend money for that which is not bread? and your labour for that which satisfieth not? hearken diligently unto me, and eat ye that which is good, and let your soul delight itself in fatness"

Isa.55:2

We all don't want to lose things of value. And often, the higher the value of something the more willing we get to pay a higher price for it.

Price is what we pay to get what we need or want. When a seller is setting up a price for something a number of things are considered. For example he or she may first want to establish how much it cost to acquire, manufacture, or ship a product. Now, we all know that anything we possess or use, whether in our homes or offices or elsewhere, was acquired at a price. In the world of business they say "there is no free lunch". That means it is impossible to get anything for nothing. But the prophet Isaiah tells us about something that we can get without money and without price:

"Ho, every one that thirsteth, come ye to the waters, and he that hath no money; come ye, buy, and eat; yea, come, buy wine and milk **without money and without price***. Wherefore do ye spend money for that which is not bread? and your labour for that which satisfieth not? hearken diligently unto me, and eat ye that which is good, and let your soul delight itself in fatness. Incline your ear, and come unto me:* **hear, and your soul shall live***; and I will make an everlasting covenant with you, even the sure mercies of David"*

(Isa.55:1-3).

How can we buy something without money and without price? In our world something without price means it is cheap. However, that is not so with the thing that God through Isaiah was inviting us to buy. It is without price not because it is cheap but because its value is too high for any price in this world! Yes, there is one thing that money cannot buy in this world and that is **life**. Isaiah 55:1-3 is actually an invitation to receive life. This can be seen in the third verse of the chapter – *"Incline your ear, and come unto me: **hear, and your soul shall live"**.*

Another important thing we should see in Isaiah 55:1-3 is that a soul can either be alive or dead. We have a **body**. In it is a **soul** which constitutes our thoughts, awareness, and consciousness. All these characteristics of the soul exist by the power of the **spirit** of life which came from God – *"And the Lord God formed man of the dust of the ground, and breathed into his nostrils the **breath of life**, and man became a **living soul"*** (Gen.2:7).

To continue *living* man was to live by the wise counsel of God; partaking of the forbidden tree would result into death. *"In the day that thou eatest thereof thou shalt surely die"* God had warned mankind (Gen.2:17).

Death

Man began his existence in the presence of God. Getting detached from that presence would result in death. It is important to note here that a thing is sustained by the substance from which it was made. As long as something is attached to the substance or place of its origin, it continues to live. In the beginning God caused plants to come forth from the soil. The soil was the origin of the plants and so as long as a plant is attached to the soil it continues to live. Its leaves and flowers will continue looking beautiful. But when a plant is removed from the soil it gets detached from its origin and it won't be long before it dies. Similarly, when God was creating fish he brought it forth from the water. Water is the place of origin for the fish and so it will continue having life as long as it is in the water. If you remove a fish from water, whether it's a great and strong fish like a shark or whale, it will die! Now when God was creating man, he first made him in his image as a spirit before *placing* him into a body of dust (Gen.1:26, 2:7). Man was created in the presence of God and was filled with the spirit of life. That spirit of life is what made the soul become conscious as a *"living soul"*. The soul in turn related to the physical world through the five senses of the flesh that was formed from the ground.

Physical death occurs when the soul, together with the spirit of life in it, leaves the body. When that happens the body cannot respond to anything because consciousness or awareness that constitutes the soul has left it.

The death of the body can be caused by the piercing of a *sword*. However, the sharp edges of a sword can only sever the soul from the body. But there is another kind of death which occurs when the spirit of life leaves the soul. If life leaves the soul all awareness of existence will cease and that would simply mean becoming non-existent. This kind of death can only be caused by God because his sword is sharper than any sword - *"For the word of God is quick, and powerful, and **sharper than any two-edged sword**, piercing even to **the dividing asunder of soul and spirit"** (Heb.4:12). And so, *"fear not them which kill the body, but are not able to kill the soul: but rather **fear him which is able to destroy both soul and body in hell"*** (Mat.10:28).That is the fate of all *"children of disobedience"*. They will burn in the Lake of Fire until they extinguish out of existence. The fire *"shall leave them neither root nor branch"* (Mal.4:1).

The lake of cleansing fire

Why will God burn souls in hell-fire? Will it be for them to just feel pain? What kind of fire will this be for it to be able to burn spiritual beings like fallen angels as well as human beings?

It is beyond the comprehension of our minds to fathom what exactly will characterize hell-fire, but one thing we know is that God uses fire for cleansing. Souls in the Lake of Fire will comprise people who had been 'loaned' the pure spirit of life but which they contaminated, so to speak, with their corrupt lifestyles. Before that life returns to God, the soul that held it will have to pass through fire. The fire will burn the vain soul until the pure spirit of life is severed from it! *"And death and hell were cast into the lake of fire. This is the second death. And whosoever was not found written in the book of life was cast into the lake of fire"* (Rev.20:14-15). When the spirit of life shall depart from all wicked souls and angels of darkness Evil would have been annihilated. It will no longer exist.

A greater loss

I hope we can all see that the greater loss to be feared in life isn't that of property or even of the body of flesh during the First Death, but the loss of one's soul which will occur to children of disobedience in the Second Death. Like the Lord Jesus admonished, *"For whosoever will save his life shall lose it: and whosoever will lose his life for my sake shall find it. For what is a man profited, if he shall gain the whole world, and* **lose his own soul***?"* (Mat.16:26). *"Blessed and holy is he that hath part in the first resurrection: on such the* **second death** *hath no power, but they shall be priests of God and of Christ, and shall reign with him a thousand years"* (Rev.20:6).

Surely nothing can be given in exchange of the soul because the life that makes it to exist is too valuable for any price we know of. It is without price. One can only buy it with his own soul using the 'currency' of *free will*. Such a decision is made possible by consciousness which in turn is caused by the spirit of life.

That our creator's will is what is right for us should be plain truth, but why is it that many people fail to perceive this? How do people afford to live through life, everyday beholding God's wonders in nature and the universe, but yet still remain blind to his purpose? In foolishness man even prefers to believe that a signal caught in space, which can exhibit a designed arrangement, would signify an intelligent source, but yet shunning the wisdom of extending the same logic to the question of why the DNA molecule in living organisms in every way functions like designed computer code!

Many people have failed to perceive the truth because they are blind and have chosen to follow the counsel of fellow blind people. Didn't the Lord warn us that *"if the blind lead the blind, both shall fall into the ditch"* (Mat. 15:14)? But well, the good news is that the blind can see!

8.

The blind can see!

*"And Jesus said, 'For judgment I am come
into this world, that they which see not might
see; and that they which see might be made
blind'"*

Joh.9:39

One day the disciples of Jesus saw a blind man and asked the Lord a question: "*Master, who did sin, this man, or his parents, that he was born blind?*" (Joh.9:2). In answering the Lord talked about light: "*As long as I am in the world, I am the light of the world*" (v.5). Why did the Lord talk about light when the disciples only asked about blindness? Well, it was for the simple reason that *sight* actually depends on *light*.

One can have a perfectly healthy eye but in the absence of light he won't be able to see. To be able to see an object, light has to fall on it and then get reflected into the eye. Inside the ball of the eye, on the *Retina*, are cells which receive the image of the object. The image is formed by patterns of the reflected light. So, an object can be right in front of you but if light doesn't fall on it you won't be able to see it. That is why no matter how close an object can be to your face, if there is completely no light you won't be able to see it. But note again that you can be in a place with enough light but if there is nothing in you to receive the light, you won't be able to see. Being able to see is thus dependent on two things – the light falling on what you have to see and having a place in you to receive the light.

As in the natural so it is in the spirit. We

come into this world enclothed in a body of flesh. The body helps us to relate with the physical world through its five senses - *sight, touch, smell, taste*, and *hearing*. But there is a consciousness within us that makes us aware of another reality which lies beyond the physical world. Some people have had glances into that spiritual world through visions or trances. But for most of the time, and for most of us, with our spirits trapped in matter, our experience of the world is similar to that of a prisoner who is locked up in a jail cell and whose perception of the external environment is only through a tiny window. This makes us strangers in our own world.

Try walking around with your eyes firmly closed. You will realize that *fear* will be your dominant feeling. You will soon become a stranger even in a place that you are already familiar with. You will suddenly wonder whether you are about to hit on a wall or trip and fall. Well did the Psalmist pray saying, "***Open thou mine eyes**...I am a **stranger** in the earth: hide not thy commandments from me*" because in the Hebrew text the word for "stranger" is *gare,* derived from *goor* which means "fear" or "afraid" (Psa.119:18-19).

Now ours is a world of foolish strangers. I once narrated this story to a church congregation:

Captured onto an aircraft you have been taken to an unknown destination. After a long flight you are dropped on a foreign land. You pull off the hood and notice different people busy doing different activities. Some are in suits and walking with briefcases into some corporate building. You see others playing football by a pitch. And a good number of others are in restaurants eating food. Which activity would you join?

"Football" answered one young man. I straightway told him that his answer was foolish: "Of all things is that what you could do? Wouldn't it be wise for you to first ask *Why* you are in that place?" Sadly, the same foolishness characterizes much of our society. We found ourselves in this big busy world. More babies are getting born every day and they grow up into the frenzy. Many people cannot pause to ask themselves this simple but yet profound question: *Why am I here?*

Like a man who buys a pen and diary from a stationary shop and immediately begins to write his stories in it, human beings find themselves equipped with the ink of life and are writing their stories on the pages of time. But if anyone dares to look closely, it's not a stationary shop we are in but an examination room! In this examination room of the world we didn't buy the book we are writing in; it was handed down to us. And although one may feel free to write what they wish, it is important to know that the book comes with a question paper that must be answered. Ignoring the pertinent questions in the paper is doing so at your own peril. Like in all academic examinations of this world, answers to the questions of life are not determined at our time of answering them but were already determined before we received the paper. Blessed are those who receive the mind and counsel of God because their lives write a story which was already established in the Book of Life. They know the foolishness of writing your own story when neither the ink nor the pages of time are yours. In this the Lord Jesus was the perfect example - "**when Christ came into the world, he said**, *'Sacrifices and offerings you have not desired, but a body have you prepared for me; in burnt offerings and sin offerings you have taken no pleasure. Then I said,* **Behold, I have come to do your will**, *O God,* **as it is written of me in the scroll of the book.**'" (Heb.10:5-7, ESV).

Anyone who does not know the will of God is blind. He or she is full of anxiety and fear. He or she is writing a life-story with closed eyes and is groping in the dark. Such a person has reduced the purpose of life to the pursuit of food, career, and pleasure. His or her life is "*a vapour that appeareth for a little time, and then vanish away*" (Jam.4:14). But the wise "*ought to say, 'If the Lord will, we shall live, and do this or that'*" (Jam.4:15).

As a believer in the will of God you have rest and should not give place to fear. The scripture admonishes you to "*not be anxious about anything, but in everything by prayer and supplication with thanksgiving let your requests be made known to God. And the peace of God, which surpasses all understanding, will guard your hearts and your minds in Christ Jesus.*" (Phi.4:6-7, ESV).

Is there hope for the blind?

The blind can see when the power of God quickens them to receive the Light. When a child of God is quickened by the Spirit of God they are born again. This spiritual birth process has something that happens which is similar to what occurs in the natural process: scientists have observed a flash of light that sparks when a sperm meets an egg and conception occurs! Surely, there is a light of life that flashes in our souls when we get born-again. That is "*the true light which lighteth every man that cometh into the world*" (Joh.1:9).

Now, the light of God that reflects into the soul of a person can never come from a creed or a motivational talk. God's light can only fall upon his Word to be reflected into a man's soul (Psa.119:19). The revealed Word of God is full of life and it is that life that can give true knowledge to mankind in this dark world - *In the beginning was the Word, and the Word was with God, and the Word was God... **In him was life; and the life was the light of men**"* (Joh.1:1, 4).

9.

The opening of eyes

"And he looked up, and said, I see men as trees, walking. After that he put his hands again upon his eyes, and made him look up: and he was restored, and saw every man clearly"

Mar.8:24-25

In the eighth chapter of Mark we read about a large crowd of people which had gathered to hear the Lord Jesus but had hungered and there was no food to eat. The Lord felt compassion. *"They have now been with me three days, and have nothing to eat...if I send them away fasting to their own houses, they will faint by the way"* he said (v.2). When the disciples heard what the Lord said, they reasoned and answered back as carnal men of the world: *"from whence can a man satisfy these men with bread here in the wilderness?"* (v.4). The eyes of the disciples could only see the few number of loaves and fish available. Spiritually they were blind to what the power of God could do.

The Lord gave thanks for the food and a miracle occurred. Not only was everyone fed but there were baskets of left-over food. Notice what happened next:

The Lord entered a ship and with his disciples they went to another place. When they reached a place called Dalmanutha some Pharisees came forth and began to question him, asking him to perform a sign. These were carnal men. Did they think God's power of signs could be wrought for mere amusement? Remember God multiplied the fish and bread because there was a need and the Lord felt compassion for the people. Well, the Lord left them and entered in the ship again to proceed to another place. Surely, where there is unbelief Jesus has no business or work to do there!

Now as they proceeded with the journey "*the disciples had forgotten to take bread, neither had they in the ship with them more than one load*" (v.14). How did the disciples handle this situation of hunger again? Did they learn anything from what had happened in the meetings they were from? Did they remember what the power of God had done?

Remembering the works of God

The psalmist said, "*I will remember the works of the Lord*" (Psa.77:11). There is power in remembering testimonies. It can ignite your faith and let God move you to higher heights in the exploits of faith. But this was not so with the disciples. As they reasoned about the lack of bread in the ship the Lord said something: "*beware of the leaven of the Pharisees, and of the leaven of Herod*" (v.15). Did the disciples understand that statement? No. Their minds were so occupied with the lack of bread and fish that when they heard the words of the Lord they thought the Lord was referring to their present worry of bread: "*And they reasoned among themselves, saying, It is because we have no bread*" (v.16). When the Lord knew about their reasonings he rebuked them for being blind: "*And when Jesus knew it, he saith unto them, Why reason ye, because ye have no bread? ... **Having eyes, see ye not?** and having ears, hear ye not? and **do ye not remember?**"* (v.17-18). The Lord went further to remind them about the recent miracle of food. He asked how much food remained after the 4000 had been fed: "*how many baskets full of fragments took ye up? And they said, Seven. And he said unto them, **How is it that ye do not understand?**"* (Mar.8:19-20).

It is always a great challenge to try to lead a person or people who are carnal because they can only live and reason as men of the world. They can never look heavenward when in trouble; they can only look up to systems of man to sustain them. Let us look at the event that happened next as the Lord travelled to illustrate more on faith in God.

Be steadfast!

God can only make a person receive sight if he or she has a desire to see. Like the psalmist prayed, "*Open thou mine eyes, that I may behold wondrous things out of thy law. I am a stranger in the earth, hide not thy commandments from me*" (Psa.119:18). Yes, God can only draw near to us when we first express a desire to draw near to him (Jam.4:8). Where there is steadfastness, focus, or intent, God reveals himself more. Where there is no steadfastness, focus, or intent, people will only have scanty ideas about God, his Word or his counsel. The voice of God will be too faint for them to hear. The revelation of his Word or doctrine will be too foggy for them to see distinctly.

When a person develops a closer walk with God he or she will experience the privilege of knowing God's counsel over things that happen around him or that may happen in other people's lives. God can then use such a person to minister or to pray for persons in need. Remember how God revealed to Abraham about what he was about to do to Sodom and Gomorrah (Gen.18:17-19).

When the Lord arrived in Bethsaida we read that, *"**they** [brought] a blind man unto him, and besought him to touch him"* (v.22). Did this blind man have a desire and the faith to get healed or he only moved along with "they" who brought him to Jesus, hoping that maybe something could happen to him? Well, the people who may have sought the Lord Jesus may have had the desire and the faith for the healing of the blind man but it was important for him to believe too. However, in our journey of faith, God can use people to help us get to a place where we can see. The good thing about this blind man is that he was willing to be led: "*And he took the blind man by the hand, and led him out of the town*"(v.23a).

When the Lord touched the eyes of the blind man something happened: "*he had spit on his eyes, and put his hands upon him, he asked him if he saw ought*" (v.23b). The poor man looked up and said "*I see men as trees walking*". Although he didn't see perfectly, what happened to his eyes must have amazed him and ignited his faith! He now had a personal experience of what the power of God could do.

When the Lord put his hands upon him again and made him to look up the Scripture says, "*he was restored and saw every man clearly*" (v.25). That is how it is worded in the King James Version Bible, but let us see a little interesting detail in other versions. In the New American Standard it says, "*again he laid his hands upon his eyes, and **he looked intently** and was restored, and began to see everything clearly*". In the Numeric English New Testament it says, "*again he laid hands upon his eyes and **he looked steadfastly** and* *was restored, and saw all things clearly"*.

The words "steadfastly" or "intently" make a big difference for what we want to illustrate in this message. With what had happened to his once dead eyes when the Lord first touched him, when he was touched the second time the man certainly had a higher expectation and no wonder he was steadfast as he looked intently, hoping to now see clearly.

See, there are many people with a distant relationship with God. They can skip prayer meetings and that doesn't bother them much. The only time they pray much is when they are in a church gathering; they simply have no personal walk with God. Although such a person may believe the truth of the word they received, what they have is a casual relationship with God. God may have done something in their lives but yet they have never lived in a manner that glorifies God. They are like those lepers who had desired healing from the Lord (Luk.17:12-19). When he commanded them to go and show themselves to the priests, as they went one of them noticed that he had been cleansed. He turned back and excitedly went to praise the Lord. *"Were there not ten cleansed? But were are the nine?"* the Lord asked.

It is important to know that the true body of Christ around the world consists of people who are steadfast in their walk with God. *"And they continued **stedfastly** in the apostles' doctrine and fellowship, and in breaking of bread, and in prayers"* (Act.2:42).

His Word, a lamp onto our feet

Living life as a spiritually blind person is a dangerous thing. One gropes in the dark wherein evil spirits lurk privily waiting on whom to devour. But when the Lord opens a person's eyes, he or she will begin to walk in the knowledge provided by the lamp of God's Word. Like the psalmist the person can testify saying, *"Thy word is a lamp unto my feet, and a **light** unto my **path**"* (Psa.119:105).

In this dark world there are so many paths that will call for your attention. If you are blind you will find yourself on any path that seems appealing. And the way of any path that is not of God is false and ultimately leads to death. Like the Scripture admonishes us, *"There is a way that seemeth right unto a man, but the end thereof are the ways of death"* (Pro.16:25). It is only when you are guided by the light of God that you will find yourself on the **way** of **truth** which leads to **life**. For born again children of God the light of God opens their eyes to the revelation of his Word and his will for their lives.

When our eyes get opened to his Word, we realise how far away we were from the truth of Scripture, or how we would have been in danger had we made a certain decision.

Testimony of seeing a hidden truth of Scripture

One day after praying I sat on a sofa which was near the door of the living room. There was a dog leaning against the door. It was crying. In a moment I went into a trance in which the cry of the dog turned into a voice that I could hear clearly. It was a speech of complaining. Few moments later my normal sense of hearing returned and there it was again, the normal cry of the dog! Many years passed and I kept this bizarre experience to myself, wondering what it meant.

One day a Jehovah Witness challenged me concerning the speaking of the serpent recorded in the third chapter of Genesis. The person said that the serpent was not a talking-animal. He reasoned that it was able to talk with Eve because it got possessed by Satan. He argued that the serpent talked in the same manner a donkey once spoke to Balaam. What the man explained seemed logical and making good sense but not when your eyes are opened to the truth of Scripture. I tried to reason with the person to show him that Genesis 3 opens with words that introduce the serpent as the most intelligent beast that was in the Garden of Eden. All my words were to no avail. But, what about the man's belief that the donkey of Balaam had spoken? Is that true?

One day whilst preaching on the Serpent-seed doctrine, like a torch which lights up a dark room and brings to light all that was obscure, my eyes got opened to see what happened to Balaam's donkey and I understood the purpose of the experience I had of hearing a dog talk.

We read in Numbers 22:28-30 that *"the LORD opened the mouth of the ass...**and the ass said unto Balaam**, Am not I thine ass, upon which thou hast ridden ever since I was thine unto this day? was I ever wont to do so unto thee? And he said, Nay."* Just how did the Lord open the mouth of the ass? Did it really speak as humans normally do? Not so! Believe it or not, if you were with Balaam on that day, all you would have heard would be the normal cry of the poor animal! But Balaam, to whom the message of the donkey was directed, heard it speak as clear as human speech! The experience I had with the dog was no different from what Balaam experienced. If there would have been another person with me by the door side, they would have only heard the cry of the dog! That is what happened one day when God spoke to the Lord Jesus; others only heard a roll of a thunder but he heard the voice of God's words clearly (Joh.12:28-29).

Testimony of God's protection

In Job 33:14 we read that *"God speaketh once, yea twice, yet man perceiveth it not."* Yes, we often don't perceive what God is trying to speak to us because of the worldly noise that often fills our minds. A mind of a person can be so congested with voices of cares of this life that God's voice only becomes a blurry shadowy thought in his mind. At a time when the Spirit would want them to pray a person may start doing something else. That prayer could have been an intercession for someone in need, or for one's own safety.

One day, around *02:00 AM* I was in deep sleep when a hand touched me on a shoulder to wake me up. I got up and got scared of what happened. I looked at my wife and she was sound asleep. I didn't bother to wake her up to tell her what had happened. I could still feel the impact of the heavy hand on my shoulder. The house was all quite and it seemed everything was fine. But the strange feeling on my heart lingered. Without thinking over it, I got up and quietly went straight to the other empty bedroom. Without turning on the lights I opened the door and right in front of the window was a burglar who was trying to break into the house!

The heavy-set man, covered in a black head-sock, was so immersed in what he was doing that he didn't see me standing and looking straight at him. Again without giving it a thought I raised my hand and spoke out loud, "What are you doing there?" The man shook in fear and staggered from the window and ran away. It is because of such moments that I have come to believe that there are so many things that happen without our knowledge but yet God is always there to protect us from harm. The experience I had may never occur again to me but it strengthened my faith to know that even when I am so deeply unconscious of God's presence, he is still there for me!

I hope we can see the danger of not perceiving what God is speaking. It is important to know that God may give a dream, vision, or word of knowledge in order to keep us away from our will, which often is blind and leads to destruction. Here are the words of Elihu, a man who was sent by God to speak to Job: "***In a dream***, *in a **vision** of the night, when deep sleep falleth upon men,* **in slumberings** *upon the bed; Then he openeth the ears of men, and sealeth their instruction,* **That he may withdraw man from his purpose**, *and hide pride from man.* **He keepeth back his soul from the pit**, *and his life from perishing by the sword*" (Job 33:15-17).

Seeking God's counsel

One day we had a strange case during a prayer meeting. A brother who used to fellowship in our congregation but had never shown up at church for some years showed up. He came with a strange prayer request. He said he was now a mental patient and would often become violent. He narrated how many times he had been admitted at a mental institution. This was a shock to all of us as we never expected such to happen to a believer. However, in a church there can be people we may regard as believers but yet are just a face in the crowd and not yet truly converted. The man pleaded for prayer and we could see his desperation. We prayed for him but nothing happened. After some days he showed up again and complained that he still experienced the terrible episodes of losing his mind. We prayed but again nothing happened!

It was about the fourth time when the man came during an evening prayer meeting and I requested him to stand in the centre and I asked other believers to be quite as I prayed:

"Lord, we have prayed all we know how to and yet this man isn't getting delivered. Please open our eyes that we may see why the evil spirit is still following him. Speak to us Lord, by vision or dream. In the name of the Lord Jesus Christ we pray, Amen."

I dismissed the gathering after the short prayer and I kept wondering if the Lord would be merciful to open our eyes concerning the man's situation. That night one sister had a dream. In the dream some people appeared to her asking, "Why do you want to help this man. He stole our things!" The sister then saw electrical appliances, radios, and other stolen goods. The following day she narrated the dream to me. It sounded odd but the man had to be told the dream.

I remember the evening he came home to hear the dream the sister had. He sat comfortably in the sofa until the dream was narrated to him. I can't forget the sight of his shivering cheeks as he struggled to explain his predicament. "But pastor, if I reveal this to the person I stole from I will be arrested…what can I do?" A family member had further confirmed to us that the man had stolen electrical goods from a certain shop. The shop owner consulted a witchdoctor and that is how the evil spell was cast upon him. That evening I told him that what to do next was all up to him.

We didn't see the brother for some time, for about two or three years. But against all our expectations he one day showed up looking so different – happy, joyous and zealous for the Lord! He testified how he had cried and agonised to God in repentance, had made things right, and that's how the madness left him. He was now spending much of his time on the streets sharing the Gospel.

Now think about how we would have still kept on casting the evil spirit out of the man to no avail had our eyes not been opened to see what the devils were holding on to. Dear friend, spiritual warfare requires that you see and know what you are fighting. And sometimes to know the will of the Lord may require that you pray and fast.

Seeking God through fasting

There was a time when the prophet Daniel had fasted for twenty-one days after which an angel came to speak to him. Surprisingly, the angel told him that the answer to his prayer had been granted the first day he started the fast. The angel had been held up from reaching Daniel on time because of a warfare that had occurred with evil angels. Dearly beloved, we may not understand everything about how the spiritual world operates but one lesson should be clear to us when we read about Daniel's experience: as human beings we live in the flesh and may not know forces which are warring against us. There may be need for us to get away from the noisy busy world and sit still to seek the Lord in prayer. There are times when one just has to fast to seek God's will over a matter. Remember when the disciples failed to cast out a demon and he told them that *"this kind goeth not out but by prayer and fasting"* (Mat.17:21).

But let us understand this: we fast not because we want God to feel sorry for our hungry stomachs but because we want to cast down *"imaginations"* and bring *"every thought to the obedience of Christ"* (2 Cor.10:3-5). We fast to keep our minds away from the noisy thoughts of the cares of this world which often hinder us from grasping what God may want us to hear. We fast to subdue our flesh. Many times our spirits may be willing to be in the presence of God but the flesh which often prefers pleasure may be standing in the way (Mat.26:41).

10.
Under one head

"This plan, which God will complete when the time is right, is to bring all creation together, everything in heaven and on earth, with Christ as head" (GNT).

Eph.1:10

There was a time when everything in creation revolved around the perfect will of God. Both the course of nature and human beings lived by God's established laws. At that time everything was right and healthy. It was man, the only creature endowed with free will and given the privilege to rule over everything else on the planet, who in trying to venture out of the perfect will of the creator threw everything out of balance.

Through time the population of the world grew. As the moral compass of man became more ossified, wickedness increased. *"Every imagination of the thoughts of his heart was only evil continually"* (Gen.6:5). Almost all human beings had become vessels of evil and hence placed themselves on the path to death. God decided to bring everything to a halt. A flood was sent to destroy everything except righteous Noah and his family.

From the three children of Noah the world was repopulated. Although evil still persisted in children of disobedience, the Lord God started a work among a people that came to be known as Israelites. Their eyes were opened to see the way that leads to life – *"Fear God, and keep his commandments: for this is the whole duty of man"* (Ecc.12:13).

God made a covenant with the Israelites. They were not to pollute themselves with the vain practices of other races. They were thus forbidden to get mixed up with the customs and traditions of other nations. God was doing an important work in them which would ultimately become a light to other nations. Various ordinances were given to Israelites to teach them obedience. In the fullness of time, Christ came to fulfil all what those practices of the law had pointed to.

When the Lord Jesus paid the price of redemption all authority was given to him by the Father. When he resurrected he gathered all saints who had been held captive by death in Sheol unto himself. From being captives of death they were now held by the power of life: *"When he ascended up on high he led captivity captive"* and ascended to heaven with those Old Testament saints (Eph.4:8, Mat.27:52-53). The whole family of heaven was thus gathered in Christ and became named after him.

The Lord commanded his disciples saying, *"All power is given unto me in heaven and in earth. Go ye therefore, and teach all nations, baptizing them in the name of the Father, and of the Son, and of the Holy Ghost. Teaching them to observe all things whatsoever I have commanded you: and, lo, I am with you always, even unto the end of the world. Amen"* (Mat.28:18). All those on Earth who die to themselves and rise in the newness of life to live by his will, signified by water baptism in the name of the Lord Jesus Christ (Act.2:38), also become part of the family and are hence also gathered into Christ.

When Jesus Christ died on the cross he paid the price for redeeming the world. By that price the *"power"* which Satan had boasted of by saying *"[it was] delivered unto me"* (Luk.4:6) was now to be given back to the Redeemer, the *"second man"* or the *"last Adam"* which is the Lord Jesus Christ. By paying that price, all *things* – both the world of Gentiles and Jews - shall be restored. Like the Lord Jesus had proclaimed before his death, *"Now is the judgment of this world: now shall the prince of this world be cast out. And I, if I be lifted up from the earth, will draw all men unto me. This he said, signifying what death he should die"* (Joh.12:32).

Good news to the Gentiles

Now, it was unthinkable that one day Gentiles, the 'unclean animals', would be cleansed from their vanities. Apostle Peter was shocked when he saw that vision of unclean animals being offered to him to eat. *"Not so, Lord; for I have never eaten any thing that is common or unclean"* he answered. But the vision spoke about a people that had never been part of the faith of the Jews. A people who were dirty with pagan beliefs and practices but now God would cleanse and graft them into the family tree.

When Peter was led to speak to a Gentile gathering he interpreted his vision to the people saying, *"Of a truth I perceive that God is no respecter of persons: But in every nation he that feareth him, and worketh righteousness, is accepted with him. The word which God sent unto the children of Israel, preaching peace by Jesus Christ: **he is Lord of all**"* (Act.10:34-36). Yes, even among the Gentiles there are those who would surrender and live by his will and hence call him Lord!

What Peter experienced had been signified in the time of Noah when both clean and unclean animals were gathered as one into the ark of safety. It was strange and unthinkable but through time Hebrew prophets had actually hinted about this great work that God would do (Gen.12:3, Isa.60:1,65:1-2, Psa.86:9-10, Rev.10:7).

As the Gospel of the resurrection of Christ spread in Israel the unexpected happened. Jews rejected the message of Salvation upon which Paul declared, *"Be it known therefore unto you, that the salvation of God is sent unto the Gentiles, and that they will hear it. And when he had said these words, the Jews departed, and had great reasoning among themselves*" (Act.28:28-29). Sad as this was, it was the working of God. He had determined a period of time during which he would only deal with the Gentiles – "*For I would not, brethren, that ye should be ignorant of **this mystery**, lest ye should be wise in your own conceits; that **blindness in part is happened to Israel, until the fullness of the Gentiles be come in**"* (Rom.11:25).

The **ultimate objective** of this mystery of God is to bring everything under the headship of Christ: "*And he made known to us the mystery of his will according to his good pleasure, which he purposed in Christ, to be put into effect when the times will have reached their fulfilment – to bring all things in heaven and on earth together under one head, even Christ*" (Eph.1:9-10, NIV). All that would come under this headship are those who willingly do so after perceiving the vanity of the world and the joy of living by his will. Yes, "*that we should be to the praise of his glory, **who first trusted in Christ**. In whom **ye [the Gentiles] also trusted**, after that ye heard the word of truth, the gospel of your salvation: in whom also after that ye **[the**

Gentiles] *believed, ye were sealed with that Holy Spirit of promise"* (Eph.1:10-13).

Notice that "trust" or "faith" in God's counsel stands at the centre of this mystery plan of God. It is important to know that the fall in Eden was caused by a desire to veer away from the perfect counsel of God. Veering away from the creator's wisdom, which is *the way of the Tree of Life* (read Pro.3:18), has been responsible for all the troubles of the world, and the only way *healing* will come to the nations of the world is by getting restored to (and eating of) that tree. That healing will occur during the millennial reign of Christ. The counsel of his Word, through his chosen kings around the world, will heal the world of all the turmoil it has gone through. *"And he showed me a pure river of water of life, clear as crystal, proceeding out of the throne of God and of the Lamb"*, apostle John narrated his vision, *"In the midst of the street of it, and on either side of the river, was there **the tree of life**, which bare twelve manner of fruits, and yielded her fruit every month: and **the leaves of the tree were for the healing of the nations**"* (Rev.22:1-2).

Dearly beloved, *"Let us hear the conclusion of the whole matter: Fear God, and **keep his commandments**: for **this is the**

whole duty of man. *For* ***God shall bring every work into judgment****, with every secret thing,* ***whether it be good, or whether it be evil****'* (Ecc.12:13-14). Amen.

Share your testimony

If God has touched you through this literature, this ministry would like to hear your testimony. Send your testimony to:
contact@andrewcphiri.com
To access sermons and other publications visit:
www.andrewcphiri.com

Notes

Notes